Household Cleaning Hacks

4th Edition

93 Crafts That Help Rid Your Home of Clutter

by Kitty Moore

Copyright © 2017 By Kitty Moore
All rights reserved. No part of this book may be reproduced in any form without permission in writing from the author. No part of this publication may be reproduced or transmitted in any form or by any means, mechanic, electronic, photocopying, recording, by any storage or retrieval system, or transmitted by email without the permission in writing from the author and publisher.
For information regarding permissions write to author at kitty@artscraftsandmore.com.
Reviewers may quote brief passages in review.

Please note that credit for the images used in this book go to the respective owners. You can view this at: ArtsCraftsAndMore.com/image-list

Kitty Moore
ArtsCraftsAndMore.com

Table of Contents

Introduction _____ 7
1. Mason Jars for Spices _____ 7
2. Hanging Pot Rack _____ 8
3. Hanging Mesh Storage for Toys _____ 9
4. Stationery Holders _____ 10
5. Plastic Boxes for Closets _____ 13
6. Mesh Bath Toy Bag _____ 14
7. Clear Plastic Cups for Batteries and Cords _____ 15
8. Belt and Jewelry Organizer _____ 16
9. Magnetic Strip for Bobby Pins and Tweezers _____ 17
10. File Box _____ 18
11. Rolling Drawers for Shoes _____ 19
12. Hanging Baskets for Linen Storage _____ 20
13. Laundry Room Racks _____ 21
14. Under the Sink Storage _____ 22
15. Ribbon Storage and Dispenser _____ 23
16. Customized Shoe Rack _____ 24
17. Books Organization System _____ 25
18. Dividers for Bill Records _____ 26
19. Hanging Shower Storage _____ 27
20. Hanging Tights Organizer _____ 28
21. Shoe Organizer Storage for Medicines _____ 29
22. Office Supplies Organizer _____ 30
23. Cleaning Rags Making and Organizing _____ 31
24. Scarf Organizer with Shower Rings _____ 32

25. Sewing Storage and Pin Cushion Using Mason Jars _____ 33
26. Spoon Holders in Closets _____ 34
27. Recycling Center for Home _____ 35
28. Christmas Ornaments Organization _____ 36
29. Button Storage in Pill Organizer _____ 37
30. Cardboard Fabric Organizing _____ 38
31. Labels for Refrigerator Doors _____ 38
32. Fabric Dresser Drawer Organizer _____ 39
33. Laundry Bucket _____ 40
34. Door Bookshelf _____ 41
35. Kitchen Utensils Rack Holder _____ 42
36. Utensil Storage Holders _____ 43
37. Easy Pot Lid Storage _____ 45
38. Children's Chore List Organizer _____ 46
39. Cable Organizers _____ 47
40. Store Garden Tools with Wooden Pallets _____ 48
41. Out of Sight Toothbrush Holder _____ 49
42. Storage Organizer for Curling Irons and Cords _____ 50
43. Jewelry Box Using Ice Cube Containers _____ 52
44. Sushi Mat Makeup Brush Organizer _____ 52
45. Modular Storage System _____ 53
46. Earring Caddy Dreamcatcher _____ 54
47. Fluffy Toy Storage Space _____ 56
48. Clever Way to Display Children's Art _____ 57
49. Magazine Storage Holder _____ 58
50. Simple Home Message Board _____ 59
51. Organize Bills in Cabinet Door Pockets _____ 63

52. Wooden Magazine Holder _____ 64
53. Easy to Make Letter Holder _____ 65
54. Recycled Cork Board _____ 66
55. Vision Board Organizer _____ 67
56. Storage Organizer Using Old Books _____ 69
57. Revamp Filing Cabinet for Storage _____ 70
58. Soda Bottles Jewelry Stand _____ 71
59. PVC Beauty Tool Holder _____ 72
60. Handy Ribbon Dispenser _____ 73
61. Handy Trash Bag Roller _____ 74
62. Nifty Fabric Organizer _____ 75
63. Thread Rack Holder _____ 76
64. Canned Food Organizer for Small Places _____ 77
65. Craft Table with Storage Shelves _____ 78
66. Quick and Easy Laundry Basket Closet _____ 80
67. Restored Drawer Storage Under Beds _____ 81
68. Covered Clothing Hangers _____ 82
69. Sewing Gadgets Organizer _____ 83
70. Fabric Covered Storage Boxes _____ 84
71. Coat Rack Using a Chair Back _____ 86
72. Ladder Blanket Holder _____ 87
73. Hanging Display Rack for Shoes _____ 89
74. Decorating an Ottoman for Storage Space _____ 90
75. Simple Holder to Store Pot Lids _____ 91
76. Handy PVC Shoe Rack _____ 92
77. Bathroom Jar Holders _____ 93
78. Framed Table Organizer _____ 94

79. Easy Container to Store Hair Accessories _____ 95
80. Storage Bin Using Recycled Tires _____ 97
81. Turn A Diaper Box into A Closet Organizer _____ 98
82. Space Saving Toilet Paper Holder _____ 99
83. Create A Magazine Rack Using a Baby Crib _____ 100
84. Gift Wrap Kitchen Stool Caddy _____ 101
85. Storage Boxes Made from Old Boxes and Sweaters _____ 103
86. Coffee Mate Storage Containers _____ 104
87. Recycle Pill Bottles to Handy Purse Storage Bottles _____ 105
88. Practical Mason Jar Toothbrush Holder _____ 106
89. Hanging Enamel Mug Organizer _____ 107
90. Creating Extra Space on Your Garage Ceiling _____ 109
91. Magnetic Makeup Board Holder _____ 110
92. Washi Tape Organizer _____ 112
93. Pencil and Pen Holders _____ 113
Conclusion _____ 114
Final Words _____ 116
Disclaimer _____ 117

Introduction

With today's fast and hectic pace, it is becoming very difficult to organize your home on a daily basis. Forget about the daily, sometimes it is impossible to even organize your home on a weekly basis. Let's accept the fact that no one likes a messy house.

You know how annoying it is when you can't find your favorite pair of shoes for that fancy party which is due to start in an hour, or struggling to get into the bathroom because the children's bath toys are all over the floor. Making your life easier just takes some organization, a little craftsmanship and the right tools to make your home clutter free and easy to manage.

Time is money. You have all heard this quote and perhaps even used it yourself. So, let's make use of this important commodity and save yourself precious time by organizing your things in a creative and useful manner.

The crafts discussed in this book are easy to make and will help you make your home more orderly, systematic and neat. So, roll up your sleeves and get going to rid the clutter that has been making your life difficult and miserable but more importantly taking up your precious time.

1. Mason Jars for Spices

Materials

- Mason jars with caps or lids
- Cardboard
- White chart paper
- Scissors
- Glue
- Permanent marker

Directions

1. Buy some mason jars. They are really cheap and just the right size to store spices. Take the lid off your mason jar, and using a marker trace the lid onto the cardboard and on to the white chart paper. Once you have marked the outline, cut out the round shapes of the lids as marked on the cardboard and chart paper.

2. Using glue, paste together the round cuttings of the white chart paper and cardboard. Write the names of spices on the round shaped cardboard cuttings by using a permanent marker. You can also write the spice code so as to help future spice purchases. Paste the round shaped cardboard cuttings on the top of the lids. Store spices in respective jars and place them in your spice drawer. You will now have a neatly organized and easy to find spice drawer.

2. Hanging Pot Rack

Materials

- Metal rods (appropriately sized)
- Hooks (to hang pots on)
- Large screw hooks with wall plugs
- Drill

Directions

1. Find a suitable location for the hanging pot rack. Make sure that you choose a location that offers no hindrance to your movement in the kitchen. Position an assembly of rods to make a rack according to your requirements. Mark the places that will hold your hanging pot rack.

2. Using a drill machine, drill the relevant holes and insert the wall plugs. Make sure that the hole is deep enough to accommodate your wall plugs. Screw in your screw hooks in to the wall plugs. Arrange your rods across the supported screw hooks.

3. Place the hooks on the rods. These hooks should be two faced so that they can hang on the rod (top hook) and hang a utensil (bottom hook). You now have a great looking hanging pot rack that will hold many of your kitchen utensils and reduce the turmoil in your kitchen drawers and on the kitchen counters.

3. Hanging Mesh Storage for Toys

Materials

- Meshed cloth
- Two hooks
- Hammer
- Two strings
- Scissors
- Needle and thread

Directions

1. Take your meshed cloth and cut into a rectangular shape according to your size requirements. Tie the two corners on the same side of the cloth together so that you have two knots on opposite ends.

2. Take a string and make two loops. The length of the loops will depend on how accessible you want the mesh cloth to be. Sew the loops onto each knot.

3. Hammer the hooks into the ceiling. Put the loops onto the two hooks and hang your meshed cloth. Put all your children's action figures and stuffed toys in the hanging mesh storage. Not only will it look great but will also save a lot of space in their room and closet.

4. Stationery Holders

Materials

- Transparent jam bottles (or something similar)
- Scissor
- Power glue
- Strings of pearls
- Spray paint (different colors)
- White paper and black marker

Directions

1. Gather all the empty jam bottles or other similar bottles in your home. Spray paint the bottles by using different colored spray paints. You can mix and match colors according to your liking. Attach small strings of pearls to these jars. Starting from the top, come down in spirals until you reach the bottom. Attach the strings to the jar with power glue.

2. Cut small pieces of white paper and according to the way you categorize your stationery, write the categories on these small white pieces of paper. For example, you can write pens and pencils, erasers and sharpeners, highlighters and miscellaneous etc.

3. Glue these papers onto each jar. Store your stationery in beautiful looking stationery holders. Now you won't have to rummage through drawers to find what you need.

I have included a bonus just for you…

FOR A LIMITED TIME ONLY – Get my best-selling book "DIY Crafts: The 100 Most Popular Crafts & Projects That Make Your Life Easier" absolutely FREE!

Readers who have downloaded the bonus book as well have seen the greatest changes in their crafting abilities and have expanded their repertoire of crafts – so it is *highly recommended* to get this bonus book today!

Get your free copy at:

ArtsCraftsAndMore.com/Bonus

5. Plastic Boxes for Closets

Materials

- Plastic boxes
- Chart paper
- Scissors
- Glue
- Marker

Directions

1. Buy some appropriately sized lightweight plastic boxes. Using a pair of scissors cut small pieces of chart paper into squares. Categorize your closet according to your requirements and write each category with a marker onto your chart paper squares. If your kids are small, you can draw pictures such as socks, toys etc. so that they can easily identify what is in each box.

2. Using glue, stick each piece of chart paper onto a plastic box. Keep the most commonly used box at a comfortable height. Put items in each respective box and now you have a perfectly manageable closet in which you can find and arrange things quickly and easily.

6. Mesh Bath Toy Bag

Materials

- Mesh cloth
- Any fabric for bag seam
- Ribbon
- Pins
- Suction hooks
- Needle / sewing machine
- Thread

Directions

1. Buy some mesh cloth. This can easily be found at a fabric or hardware store. Cut two equally sized mesh cloths according to your requirements and pin together. Sew the two pieces of cloth together with a sewing machine or needle and thread. Remember to leave one side open.

2. Along the edges of the bag, sew on your fabric so that it becomes a binding covering the seams. This will ensure that your bag becomes more durable. Make two loops of ribbon and sew them onto either side of the opening of your bag. These loops will be used for hanging the bag.

3. Buy a couple of suction hooks. You can easily buy them from a hardware store or any super store. Put the two suction hooks on the wall and hang the bag on them. Once your children have finished playing in the tub, place all their wet and dripping toys into the bag. Now the toys are easily accessible for your children at bath time and of course you will have a neat and tidy bathroom.

7. Clear Plastic Cups for Batteries and Cords

Materials

- Clear plastic cups
- Marker
- Glue
- Scissors
- Chart paper

Directions

1. Buy a few clear plastic cups or use plastic cups that you have at home. With a scissor, cut the chart paper into small rectangular or square pieces, which will become labels.

2. On the pieces of paper, write the names of different things you want to store in the cups. For example, AA batteries, LAN cables etc.

3. Using the glue, stick the small pieces of paper on different cups. Put all your cords and batteries into their respective cups. Your cords will no longer be jumbled in knots and you will always know which batteries are still usable.

8. Belt and Jewelry Organizer

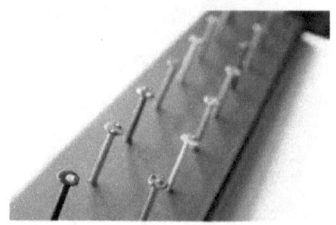

Materials

- Wooden sheet
- Hooks or wooden pegs
- Glue
- Screws and wall plugs
- Saw
- Drill

Directions

1. Cut the wooden sheet into small strips according to your size requirement. Choose a suitable place, such as a hall in your house or the back of your bedroom door.

2. Make holes in the wall using a drill, deep enough to accommodate the wall plugs. Secure the wooden strips onto

the wall using screws. If attaching your wooden sheets to the back of a door, use a screwdriver to attach with screws.

3. Mount the hooks onto the wooden strips. Make sure that you choose the right sized screws that will stay within the wood's width. You can also use wooden pegs instead of hooks. If using wooden pegs, attach into the correct places with glue that is suitable for use on wood. Hang your favorite belts and jewelry on the hooks. Now you have a place to display your jewelry and you won't have to worry about jewelry or belt damage that happens when kept in your drawer.

9. Magnetic Strip for Bobby Pins and Tweezers

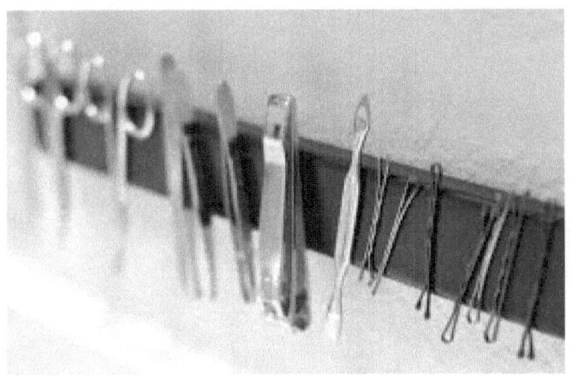

Materials

- Magnetic strip
- Double sided tape

Directions

1. Buy a magnetic strip from your local hardware store. They are usually quite cheap.

2. Choose a suitable location for the magnetic strip such as space above the bathroom mirror etc. Secure your magnetic strip with double sided tape

3. Place all your bobby pins, needles, tweezers etc. On the magnetic strip. In this way, they won't get lost and you will be able to find them easily.

10. File Box

Materials

- Plastic box
- Labels
- Marker
- Cardboard
- Scissors
- Glue

Directions

1. Take any empty plastic or cardboard box in your home. Measure the dimensions of your box and mark cardboard accordingly. Add on an extra inch on the sides. Cut cardboard separations for the box.

2. Fold over the additional inch on both sides and paste inside the box with glue. Make sure to leave space between each piece of cardboard so that you have partitions.

3. Label each file and insert one file in each partition. Make sure that the label is clearly visible when the file is in the box. This will assist finding the correct file quickly. This file box can be used to hold your home office files or if you are a student, your homework.

11. Rolling Drawers for Shoes

Materials

- Wood
- Saw
- Measuring tape
- Nails or screws
- Hammer
- Wheels

Directions

1. Measure the space between the floor and the bottom of your bed. Depending on the size of the drawer you need, mark the dimensions of the drawer on your wood. There will be 4 sides and a base. Remember to take into account the height of your wheels, as this will dictate the height of your drawer.

2. Using a saw cut your wood or you can give the hardware store the dimensions and they will cut to size. Join all the pieces of wood in the shape of a drawer. Using nails or screws, attach the wheels on all four corners of the drawer. Make sure that you choose wheels that can bear the weight.

3. Make small wood partitions inside the drawer for better organization. Put all your extra shoes inside and wheel the drawer under your bed. Take out your shoes only when you need them. Not only will this handy drawer save you space but you will no longer having shoes lying around or piled into a closet.

12. Hanging Baskets for Linen Storage

Materials

- Nesting baskets
- Nails
- Hammer

Directions

1. Buy different sized nesting baskets. If you are lucky, you might find them for less than $10 each. Find a good spot to install these baskets. For example, above the bathroom seat.

2. Using nails attach the baskets to the wall, making sure that you keep the open face of basket towards you.

3. Put linen and other such items into the baskets. Now you have created space for different items that otherwise would be taking up closet space that could be used for other essentials in your bathroom.

13. Laundry Room Racks

Materials

- Metal racks
- Screws
- Drill

- Brackets
- Plastic baskets

Directions

1. Buy some suitably sized metal racks from a hardware store. These racks are great to use above your washing machine. Mark the correct area, drill holes and insert wall plugs. Attach the racks to the wall.

2. Put multi-colored plastic baskets on the racks. Store all your laundry supplies including detergent in the baskets. Not only will you save a lot of space but the baskets will also help you to organize your laundry more efficiently.

14. Under the Sink Storage

Materials

- Hanging rod
- Screws
- Screw driver
- Plastic baskets
- Drill

Directions

1. Measure the space under your sink and buy an appropriate sized hanging rod. Mark the points where you need to drill holes. Drill and insert wall plugs.

2. Screw the rod to the wall. Hang any detergent and soap spray bottles on the hanging rod. Place small plastic baskets under the hanging rod.

3. All other supplies can be put inside these plastic baskets. Now you have access to unused space and have organized your things in a very systematic and orderly manner.

15. Ribbon Storage and Dispenser

Materials

- Plastic basket with holes
- Plastic dowel rod

Directions

1. Purchase a plastic basket with holes. Buy a plastic dowel rod that is the approximate width of the basket. Insert the one side of the rod through a hole in the basket.

2. Put the ribbon spools on the plastic rod and insert the other end of the rod through a hole. This will allow the ribbon to rotate on the dowel rod.

3. Pass the ends of ribbons through different holes, which will make it easy to pull out the ribbon of your choice.

16. Customized Shoe Rack

Materials

- Wood
- Saw
- Drill
- Screws
- Sandpaper
- Measuring tape
- Hammer

Directions

1. First of all, decide on the place where you want to keep the shoe rack. You'll probably want to keep it near to the entrance of your house. Measure the available space and mark the measurements of shoe rack on your wood.

2. Cut the outer frame according to the measurements and join the frame together. Drill two holes on either side and secure tightly with screws. Once the outer frame is made, make different sized compartments inside the shoe rack.

3. Make some of the compartments small and the others a little larger. Place your shoes in the rack. Now you can easily manage your shoes and you won't have to go through the hassle of looking in each shoebox.

17. Books Organization System

Materials

- Plastic baskets
- White chart paper
- Marker
- Glue
- Scissors

Directions

1. Buy some small plastic baskets that can store books in. Using the chart paper cut out labels. Write the different book categories on the labels. For example, children books, cookery books etc.

2. Attach these labels to the baskets and place the relevant books into each basket.

3. Place the basket underneath your desk or in a suitable area, saving you from having to search for books when needed because you have now created an organized and manageable book storage system.

18. Dividers for Bill Records

Materials

- File
- Cardboard
- Colored chart paper
- Scissors
- Glue

Directions

1. Take a file and cover it with a wrapping paper. Cut your cardboard into an A4 size except make the width a half an inch wider (this will become your file divider)

2. Cut small labels of different colors from the chart paper. Paste the labels on your file divider at different intervals. Label them according to your requirements. Insert the dividers into your file.

3. Organize all your bills under each labeled file divider. As new bills arrive, you can file them away immediately instead of them cluttering your home.

19. Hanging Shower Storage

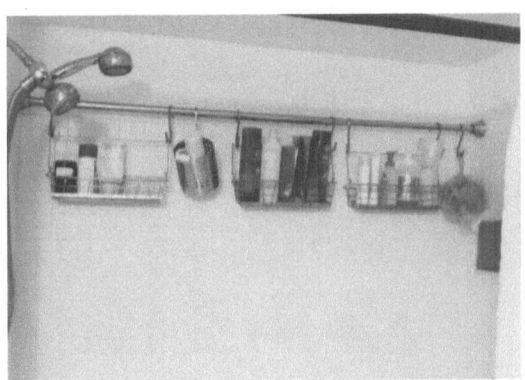

Materials

- Drill
- Screws and wall plugs
- Shower rod
- Two sided hooks
- Screwdriver
- Plastic baskets

Directions

1. Mark the spot where you want to fit the rod. Preferably you should put it beside the shower rod that has curtains on it as this space is unutilized and is within reach when taking a shower.

2. Drill holes in the wall and insert wall plug. Screw in the rod. Place the two-sided hooks on to the rod. Hang small sized plastic baskets on the hooks. Preferably baskets that have holes in them so as to eliminate any excess water. These baskets become a perfect place to store oils, shower gels, shampoos and other shower items.

20. Hanging Tights Organizer

Materials

- Wood
- Drill
- Screws and wall plugs
- Wooden clothespins
- Glue gun

Directions

1. Decide on an appropriate place to hang your tights. A good idea can be the back wall of your closet or behind your bedroom door. Take the measurements and purchase a piece of wood according to your requirements.

2. Mark the area where you want to place the hanging organizer. Drill the marked spots and insert wall plugs. Insert screws to fix the wood to the wall.

3. Using a wood glue attach your wooden clothespins to the wood at intervals and allow to dry. Hang your tights on the clothespins. No longer do you need to rummage through tights stuffed in your closet drawers and no more problems in finding the right tights!

21. Shoe Organizer Storage for Medicines

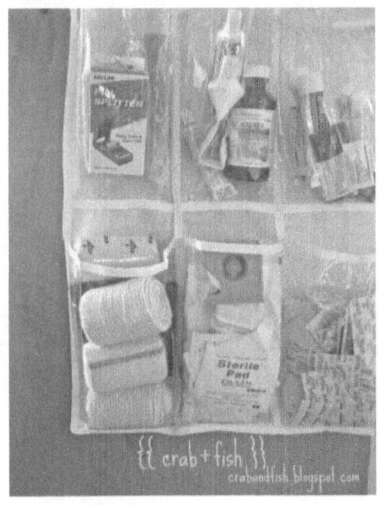

Materials

- Hammer
- Nails

- Shoe organizer

Directions

1. This is a very easy solution to managing all your cluttered and hard to find medicines. Simply buy a shoe organizer that has small compartments.

2. Decide where you want to hang the shoe organizer and mark the area. As long as your children can't reach, a good place could be the door of your storage cupboard.

3. Hammer nails into the marked spots. Hang the shoe organizer on the nails and put all your medicines in different compartments. An easy and accessible way to store medicines!

22. Office Supplies Organizer

Materials

- Small plastic containers (varying sizes)
- Frame (for holding containers)
- Measuring tape

Directions

1. This is an easy, cheap and effective way to organize your office supplies. Buy a few small plastic containers of varying sizes.

2. Estimate the amount of space the containers will take in your drawer by arranging them and measuring the area they cover. Make a suitable frame for the area covered or you can buy a suitably sized frame from the market.

3. Put all your boxes inside the drawer. Fill each container with different office supplies. Your stationary is now organized and you will be able to find what you want quickly and easily.

23. Cleaning Rags Making and Organizing

Materials

- Old T-shirts
- Dustbin
- Sharp box knife
- Solid cutting board / workbench
- Bolts
- Wood
- Drill

- Hammer

Directions

1. Take a couple of old T-shirts. Cut each shirt one by one. Fold the T-shirt in half and cut it. Then again fold the two pieces in half and cut them. Now you have 4 rags from one T-shirt.

2. Take wooden piece on which you can bolt your dustbin rag holder. Use hammer and nails to put up the wooden piece against the wall. Drill on one side of dustbin and make a hole on the bottom of other side. Using nuts and bolts tighten the dustbin onto the wooden frame. Put all your rags inside the dustbin and you can easily pull one out from the bottom when needed.

24. Scarf Organizer with Shower Rings

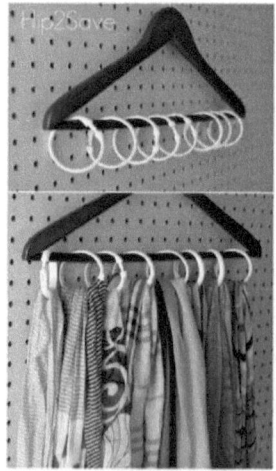

Materials

- Hanger
- Shower rings

Directions

1. Buy shower rings from a local hardware store. They would cost around a dollar or so. Take a hanger and insert the shower rings onto the hanging rod.

2. Put one scarf in each ring until you have around 8-10 scarfs on each hanger. Hang in your closet or wherever else is suitable. Your scarves are now easy to find and they could also act as a nice decoration.

25. Sewing Storage and Pin Cushion Using Mason Jars

Materials

- Mason jars with removable lids
- Stuffing
- Fabric scraps
- Scissors
- Hot glue

Directions

1. Trace the outline of the lid on chart paper and add on an inch all round. Cut the fabric according to your tracing. Using hot glue, secure some stuffing on the lid and cover the stuffing with the cut fabric.

2. Glue down stray ends of the fabric to the inside of lid. Now you have a cushion to put all your pins when sewing. Not only will your jar serve as a pincushion but you can also put sewing supplies inside the jar.

26. Spoon Holders in Closets

Materials

- Hammer
- Nails
- Plastic hooks
- Power glue (if needed)

Directions

1. Buy plastic hooks from a hardware store. Mark the points on the inside of your kitchen closet where you want to hang your spoons.

2. Hammer each hook into the closet. If your closet is made of plastic, you can use power glue to attach hooks to the inside of

the closet. Hang your spoons on the hooks and create additional space in kitchen drawers.

27. Recycling Center for Home

Materials

- Plastic cans
- Pegboard
- White chart paper
- Scissors
- Glue

Directions

1. Buy a pegboard and some plastic cans from a local hardware store. They are quite cheap and you will find them easily. Attach the pegboard to a wall.

2. Mount the plastic cans on the pegboard. Cut small labels from the chart paper. Categorize your recycling cans and write respectively on the labels.

3. Glue the labels onto the cans. You can also use the pegboard for hanging other things such as scissors, nail cutters etc.

Recycle things daily, you will have much less mess to deal with and of course you will be helping save the planet at the same time!

28. Christmas Ornaments Organization

Materials

- Plastic cups
- Plastic baskets

Directions

1. Buy some plastic cups, the red ones that you usually see in fraternity parties would do nicely. Additionally, they would give a Christmas touch and color to your ornament storage.

2. If you have any empty plastic baskets, and arrange the cups in rows and columns. Once the cups have been arranged, put Christmas ornaments inside the cups.

3. If you have lots of ornaments, you can stack multiple baskets. Make sure that your baskets are such that each top basket fits in the bottom basket. Store the baskets in your garage or closet.

29. Button Storage in Pill Organizer

Materials

- Pill organizer
- White chart paper
- Scissors
- Glue
- Marker

Directions

1. A pill organizer is a great place to store your buttons. They are relatively inexpensive. If you want, use the chart paper to create labels for your buttons.

2. Stick the labels onto the compartments using glue. Put all your buttons into different compartments. If your pillbox is transparent, you can easily see which types of buttons are in which compartment. No more hassle in storing or finding buttons.

30. Cardboard Fabric Organizing

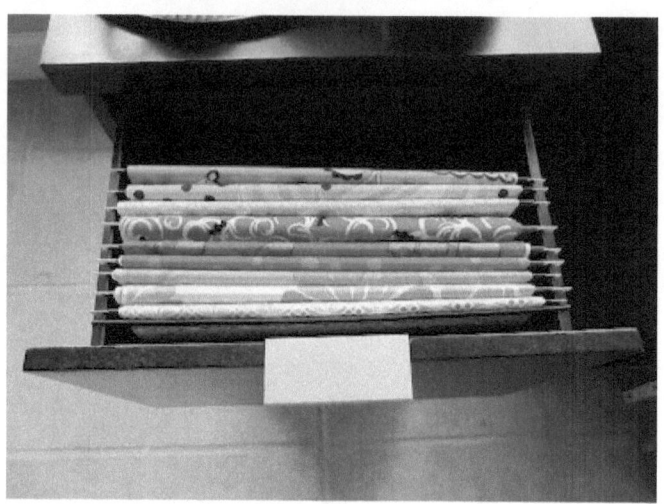

Materials

- Cardboard
- Plastic tote / magazine rack

Directions

1. If you keep a lot of fabrics in your closet and always find it difficult to find a specific one, this is a great idea. Take a few pieces of cardboard that would suit your storage area. Wrap each fabric around each piece of cardboard.

2. Keep the wrapped fabrics in a magazine rack, tote bag or if you prefer, they can be kept in a closet. Now you have easy access to each fabric when you need it and just replace after use

31. Labels for Refrigerator Doors

Materials

- Chart paper
- Plastic sheet (PVC)
- Double sided stick on
- Scissors
- Permanent marker

Directions

1. Your refrigerator can be clutter free with these simple labels. Using your chart paper, cut out small labels. Write on the labels according to your requirements using a permanent marker.

2. Cover each label with PVC sheet so that moisture in the refrigerator does not damage the labels.

3. Attach the labels to the refrigerator door using double-sided stickers. Now each member in the family knows where to put what.

32. Fabric Dresser Drawer Organizer

Materials

- Fabric bucket organizers

Directions

1. You can easily get these fabric organizers from a super store. They cost between $5-10. Put them in the dresser drawer. Separately place items such as socks, pony tails etc. in each fabric bucket. Your dresser drawer will be perfectly organized and you will be able to find things quickly and easily.

33. Laundry Bucket

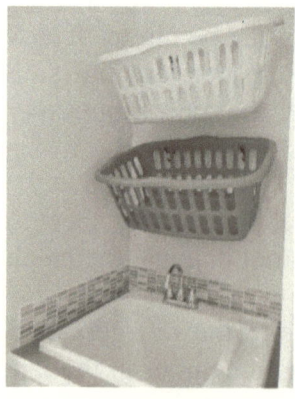

Materials

- Plastic buckets

- Steel hooks
- Hammer

Directions

1. A laundry bucket in every room can reduce your clothes mess tremendously. Insert hooks onto the wall at a convenient space in the bedroom.

2. Hang the plastic bucket on the hook. Tell your family to put their dirty laundry in the bucket. When the bucket is full, remove the bucket and take the clothes to the laundry. No more dirty clothes will be left lying around your home!

34. Door Bookshelf

Materials

- Wood
- Saw
- Nails
- Hammer
- Measuring tape
- Sliding glass

Directions

1. The first step is to measure the dimensions of your door. Using the saw cut your wood and build a frame according to your door size. Make sure that the wood is light in weight.

2. Make shelf-using wood and store your books on these shelves. Put sliding glass in front of the bookshelf so that your books do not fall when you open or close the door. These bookshelves are ideal for sliding doors. Your books finally found a place where they can sit in peace, which is if you do not read!

35. Kitchen Utensils Rack Holder

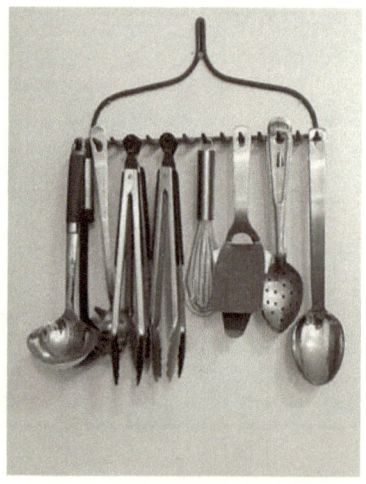

Materials

- Rake
- Drill and drill bit
- Screw and wall plug (the size should allow for the width of your rake)
- Screw driver

Directions

1. Purchase a rake from your hardware store or if you want an old-fashioned rake find one at a second-hand store. Locate an appropriate position to hang your rake in your kitchen.

2. Mark the position and drill a hole with your drill. Make sure that the hole is deep enough to accommodate your wall and insert the wall plug.

3. Attach your rake to the wall. Hang your most commonly used utensils on the hooks of the rake. Cooking has now become that much easier with your utensils close at hand.

36. Utensil Storage Holders

Materials

- Cast iron filigree with hooks
- Drill and drill bit
- Screws and wall plugs
- Screw driver
- Small wooden chopping boards
- Chart paper

- Pins
- Fabric
- Needle and thread
- Small nails and hammer
- Ribbon or patterned trimming
- Glue
- Scissors
- Thin rope

Directions

1. Purchase from your hardware store or online cast iron filigree motifs. They must have hooks attached to them. Identify where you would like to hang your storage holders and mark.

2. Drill holes in to the marked area and insert your wall plug. Screw your cast iron filigree on to the wall. Measure the size of your cutting board (lengthwise, excluding the hole at the top of the board).

3. Draw the measurements on your chart paper but increase the width by half. Cut out the shape (this becomes your pattern). Pin your pattern on to your fabric and cut out the shape.

4. Neaten the edges of your fabric by folding over each edge of your fabric and sew. Place the fabric on your board, slightly ruching the bottom section and attach to the board with small nails.

5. Along the side of your fabric (lengthwise), glue on your trimming. Hang your board on the hooks of your filigree holder. If you want the boards at different lengths, make a loop with rope, knot and hand the board on the hook.

6. Fill your newly made pockets with utensils, making them easily accessible and handy to use whilst adding a touch of beauty to your kitchen.

37. Easy Pot Lid Storage

Materials

- Stainless steel rods with curved edges in appropriate size
- Fitting to insert rod
- Pencil
- Screw driver
- Screws and wall plugs

Directions

1. Measure the inside of a kitchen cabinet and purchase stainless steel rods in the appropriate length.

2. Mark where you would like your rods to be placed. Screw in the fittings and attach rods.

3. Place your pot lids between the cabinet door and the rod, with the pot handle resting on your rod. Now the right size pot lid can be easily found and you will have extra space in your pot drawers to stack your pots.

38. Children's Chore List Organizer

Materials

- Cork Notice Board (sized to your family requirements)
- Tacks
- Chart paper (white and one color for each child)
- Magnetic boards (one per child)
- Small magnets (one color per child)
- Marker
- Double sided tape
- Glue

Directions

1. Purchase a cork notice board as per the size required. Attach with double sided tape to a wall that is visible to your family, perhaps in the kitchen or mudroom. On each colored paper write down or type the name of each child. On the white paper write or type the days of the week and a task for each day. Glue the child's name at the top of each task page and place on the corkboard with tacks.

2. Beneath the corkboard, attach the magnetic boards to the wall with double-sided tape. On your colored paper write each child's name and paste to the top of the board. On a separate piece of paper write the following headings: Good Morning, To Do and Done. Below Good Morning write the activities you expect them to do. For example, get dressed, brush teeth, tidy room etc.

3. Underneath the list make another heading – Good Night. Here too you will list activities. For example, homework, reading, chores etc. Depending on how many activities you list, have the same amount of magnets. As each child completes their activities, they will move the magnet to the done side of the board. Children need routine and with a quick glance they can see what they need to do and feel proud as they accomplish each task. This will also eliminate you having to nag your children to do things.

39. Cable Organizers

Materials

- Used toilet rolls
- Washi tape in different colors and patterns
- Scotch tape

- Chart paper
- Glue
- Plastic container

Directions

1. Collect your used toilet rolls. Cut strips of washi tape the circumference of the toilet roll. Place the strips of washi tape over the sticky parts on the toilet roll and join with scotch tape. Cut small pieces of chart paper to make labels and on each label, write where each cable is used. For example, computers, DVD player, hard drive etc. Neatly roll up each cable and insert into the toilet roll. Remember to glue the relevant label to the correct toilet roll. Place your new cable organizers in a plastic container saving you time untangling and hunting for the right cable when you next need it.

40. Store Garden Tools with Wooden Pallets

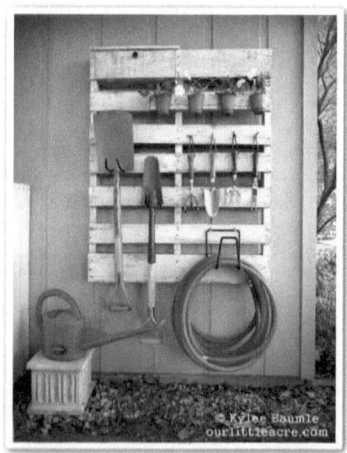

Materials

- 2 Wooden Pallets
- Hinges
- Magnetic strips

- Power glue
- Small door knob
- Power screw driver
- Saw
- Steel brush
- Metal hooks
- Screws
- Wood screws
- Nails
- Kitz primer and brush

Directions

1. Find an old wooden pallet at your local nursery of super store. On the one pallet, cut the wood on the top left hand between the supporting frames. Do the same to the other pallet except that you need two pieces of the same size in order to make a door.

2. On the original pallet, screw one piece of wood on the top of where you had cut. Attach hinges to this section. Attach the opposite side of the hinges to the other piece of cut wood. You will now have made a closed compartment. Attach the magnets on the door and the pallet so as to securely close your compartment. Fasten the doorknob to the door.

3. Brush the pallet with the steel brush to remove dirt and splinters. Paint with Kitz primer to give a whitewashed look. Decide where you would like to place your garden tools and hammer in a few nails and your hooks to facilitate. Attach your pallet to the side of a building or tree that is rain free. If you are really feeling adventurous pot plants can also be hung on your garden pallet. Easy access to your garden tools can now make working in your garden a pleasure.

41. Out of Sight Toothbrush Holder

Materials

- Rotary tool
- Sanding drum
- Woodcutting bit
- Pencil and ruler

Directions

1. Just below the head of your toothbrush, measure the dimensions of the toothbrush handle. Mark these measurements on the inside of your medicine cabinet (should be a rectangular shape with the opening being at the edge of the shelf).

2. Using your rotary tool cut the sides of the shape, and the woodcutting bit for the back part of the rectangle. Sand the cut area. Slip the toothbrushes in to the open slots, leaving your washbasin clean and uncluttered.

42. Storage Organizer for Curling Irons and Cords

Materials

- Screw hooks
- PVC pipe – 2 inches in diameter (curling irons)
- PVC pipe – 1 ½ inches in diameter (cords)
- Double sided tape
- Hacksaw
- Vise or clamp
- Marker

Directions

1. Purchase PVC piping from your local hardware or super store. Ask your hardware store to cut the piping; if unable you can cut at home. Each 2-inch pipe must be 5 inches in length. If at home, mark the length of the pipe accordingly. Each 1 ½ inch pipe must be 3 inches in length. Mark the pipe accordingly. Secure pipe in a vise or clamp and saw at your marked areas. Attach the pipes to the inside of your vanity door, next to one another with double sided tape.

2. Place your curling iron into the 5-inch pipe and mark where the handle would have to be supported. Insert the screw hook at the marked area. The cord can be neatly folded and placed in to the smaller holder whilst the curling iron will go in to the

other holder. Now you will have more space in your drawers or dressing table for other things.

43. Jewelry Box Using Ice Cube Containers

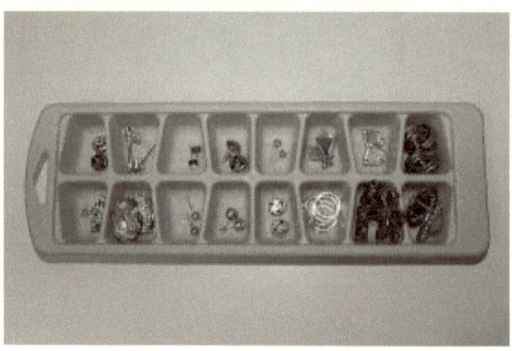

Materials

- Hard plastic ice cube trays

Directions

1. Organize your jewelry – rings, necklaces, earrings etc. so that each item has its own home within the cube. If need be, you can stack one tray on top of the other making it a multi layered jewelry box. This of course will save you space. Your ice cube jewelry box can be housed in a drawer or on a table. Now you will be able to find exactly what you need with a single glance.

44. Sushi Mat Makeup Brush Organizer

Materials

- Sushi mat
- Thick elastic
- Needle and thread
- Ribbon

Directions

1. Open your sushi mat and check the length of your longest make up brush. Mark where the middle of your brush would be and it is on this line that the elastic will be placed. Wrap the elastic through the first two sticks and fold underneath the remaining elastic. Secure the elastic with a few stitches. Weave the elastic through the sticks at different intervals, making space for a variety of sizes.

2. At the end of the mat, wind the elastic around the last few sticks and once again secure with a few stitches. Place you brushes in the open spaces, roll up the mat and tie with a pretty ribbon. Now your brushes are all in one place, easy to view and use. If you are going on holiday, roll up and pop into your case saving you space to put in those extra goodies you want to take with.

45. Modular Storage System

Materials

- Prant or chipboard boxes (variety of sizes and shapes)
- Paint of your choice (can use different colors)
- Paint brush
- Stationery clamps

Directions

1. Paint the inside of some of the boxes. Dependent on your color scheme it can be in pastels or bright bold colors for children. Position the boxes in a modular fashion and to your requirements. Clip the side of two boxes together with a stationery clamp. This is a simple, easy and effective way to transform spaces with designer storage units.

46. Earring Caddy Dreamcatcher

Materials

- Embroidery hoop
- Embroidery floss (variety of colors)
- Metallic spray paint
- Earrings
- Newspaper
- Wood glue
- Pliers
- Nail

Directions

1. Separate your embroidery hoop. Place on a piece of newspaper and spray with paint. Leave until dry. The fastener on the outside hoop one can either leave on or it can be removed with pliers. If you chose to remove, glue together the two ends with wood glue and spray.

2. Tie your embroidery floss to the top of your hoop ensuring that you leave sufficient floss to make a loop for hanging. Pull the floss 3 inches to the right and wrap around the hoop. Continue doing this until you have created a 7-sided heptagon.

3. Take either the same floss or a different color and continue to make heptagons but starting at the center of the heptagon you have just completed. Repeat this pattern until such time as your hoop is covered in a web of floss. Cut the floss and tie in a

knot. Know the loop that is at the top of your hoop. Hammer a nail into the wall or an area where you would like to display your dreamcatcher. All that is left, is to hand your earrings onto your dreamcatcher and viola, you have something beautiful to look at but also a safe space to hang your special earrings.

47. Fluffy Toy Storage Space

Materials

- Bookshelf
- Four bungee cords
- Drill and ½ inch spade drill bit
- Scissors
- Marker
- Tape measure
- Paint (optional)

Directions

1. Remove the shelves from the bookshelf. You can either leave in its natural finish or paint according to taste or color scheme.

Depending on the size of your bookshelf, make a mark 2 inches from the edge of either side. Thereafter mark every 4 inches. Do this on the top as well as the bottom of the bookshelf.

2. Drill holes at each marking. Slide the hook of the bungee cord to the one end and cut off the knot. Now you will be able to slide off the two hooks and the tag. Thread the knotted side of the bungee cord through the bottom of your bookshelf. Line up with the corresponding hole above, thread through the hole pulling tight and make a knot. Repeat this step until all the cords are in place.

3. Burn the ends of the cord so that is does not unravel. Place all your children's fluffy toys in their new home. Your children will have lots of fun finding their toys and packing away will be fun too.

48. Clever Way to Display Children's Art

Materials

- Large wooden letters spelling ART
- Clipboards

- Drill
- Screws and wall plugs
- Paint of choice
- Paint brush
- Newspaper
- Double sided tape
- Tape measure
- Marker
- Screwdriver

Directions

1. Paint the clipboards and letters in a color of your choice. Leave to dry.

2. Choose a suitable location like a playroom where you would like to display your children's art.

3. Using double-sided tape, stick your letters on the wall.

4. Depending on how many clipboards you want, mark their position on the wall.

5. Each clipboard is to have 4 holes, one for each corner. Mark the same positions on your clipboard.

6. Drill holes in the marked positions and insert wall plug.

7. Screw your clipboards into position. Now you have a handy area to clip all your children's art, they will be proud and so will you!

49. Magazine Storage Holder

Materials

- Filigree wall bracket
- Tin bucket
- Screws and wall plugs
- Drill and concrete bit
- Marker
- Tape measure

Directions

1. Purchase a filigree wall bracket from your hardware store or nursery. Find a suitable location like next to your bed, playroom etc. Mark the position of the holes. Drill holes and insert wall plugs. Screw the bracket on to the wall.

2. Hang a tin bucket hang on the bracket or purchase one a vintage bucket from a second-hand store. All that remains is for you to fill the bucket with your favorite magazines, leaving your bedside neat and tidy.

50. Simple Home Message Board

Materials

- Mirror with wooden frame (size depends on your requirements and space)
- 3 Inch strip of wood (2 inches longer than the width of frame)
- Hacksaw
- Screw and wall plugs
- Drill and bit
- Wood glue
- Colored markers

Directions

1. Measure the width of you frame and mark on the strip of wood. Measure two extra pieces of I inch each and mark. Cut along the marked lines.

2. Glue the long strip of wood in the middle of the bottom half of your frame (this becomes a shelf to hold markers). The two extra pieces of wood are glued to the side of the shelf as well as the mirror.

3. Position the mirror in your preferred location and mark. Drill a hole and insert wall plugs. Screw in the screw that will hold

the mirror. Place colored markers on the shelf. Have fun writing mirror messages for your family or reminders of things you need to do or buy.

Check out Kitty's books at:

ArtsCraftsAndMore.com/go/books

51. Organize Bills in Cabinet Door Pockets

Materials

- 8-1/2-inch x 11-inch piece scrap book paper (as many as you require)
- Laminator (if you have)
- Laminator pouches 3 millimeters thick
- Re-closable fasteners (8 per pocket)
- Paper trimmer or scissors
- Chalkboard labels
- Chalk marker
- Heavy duty page protectors and scotch tape (if you don't have a laminator)

Directions

1. Cut 2 inches off the length of your craft paper. Fold the length of your paper in half with the printed section facing outwards. Put two pieces of paper in your laminating pouch, and laminate.

2. Trim around 3 sides of the pocket, leaving a little space on the edges to prevent the laminate from separating over time. Trim the top edge where the papers meet in line with the paper.

3. In each corner, place a re-closable fastener (soft side). Stick on your chalkboard label and write on the categories. If you don't have a laminator, place your folded craft paper into a page protector and cut to size. Seal the paper to the plastic with scotch tape.

4. Decide which cabinet you want your bill organizers and mark in line with the fasteners on the pockets. Adhere the other side of the fastener to the cabinet (4 pieces) and hang on the door. Place your bills or receipts in your organizer pockets and add or take out when you need.

52. Wooden Magazine Holder

Materials

- Porch trim brackets
- 2 Pieces wood cut to the width and length of brackets
- Hacksaw
- Wood glue
- Paint and brush

Directions

1. Decide the length that you require for your magazine rack and purchase wood (the width and length of the rack is in line with that of a standard magazine).

2. Cut wood according to your size. Paint the wood and brackets in the color of your choice. Glue the base and back section together. Make sure that you have something to support the back until the glue is dry.

3. Glue the brackets to the L shaped frame at intervals and glue is dry. This holder is ideal for those special magazines that you would like to keep or make reference to on a regular basis.

53. Easy to Make Letter Holder

Materials

- Small hardcover book
- Craft glue
- Sponge brush
- Ruler
- Utility knife

Directions

1. Separate the pages into equal sections and mark with a piece of paper. Work in one section at a time and apply glue to the inside seam.

2. Spread glue evenly across the seam with the sponge brush. Roll the first section towards the seam, press and hold firmly in place. Continue with the same method until you have glued each section.

3. After all the glue has dried, use the knife to remove any excess glue. Although this is a practical solution to keeping all your post together, it also becomes a beautiful display item in your entrance hall.

54. Recycled Cork Board

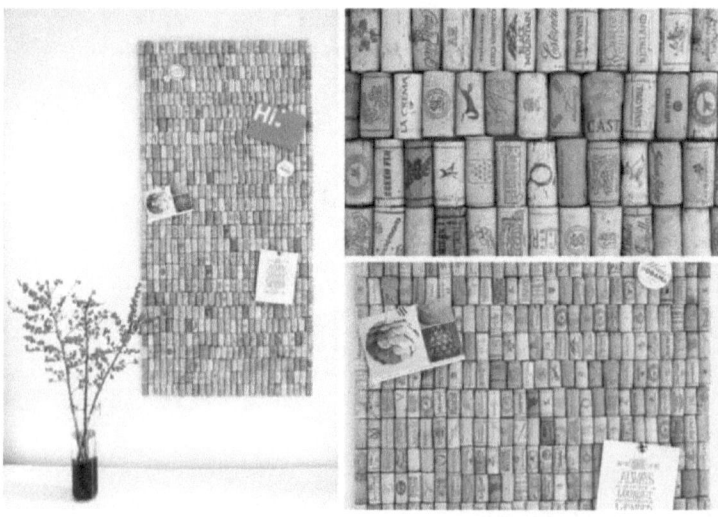

Materials

- Piece of thin wood board
- Used wine corks

- Hot glue
- Nails
- Hammer
- Tacks

Directions

1. Cut a piece of thin board according to your requirements. Wine corks come in different sizes, so sort in to similar sizes.

2. Glue the corks horizontally across your board in a row. Continue until the whole board has been covered.

3. Attach to the wall in your preferred location. Place all your notes and reminders on to your recycled but attractive cork board.

55. Vision Board Organizer

Materials

- Piece of board as per your requirements
- Paint
- Paint brush
- Thumb tacks
- Gift bags
- Stationary clamps
- Glue
- Nails
- Hammer

Directions

1. Find a suitable location for your vision board like a bedroom or study. Measure the size and purchase your board. Your hardware store should be able to cut to size. Paint in a color of your choice.

2. Around the edge of the board, push or hammer in your thumbtacks. In the center section of your board, arrange your gift bags and mark.

3. Glue the black of the bag and paste the bags on to your board. Along either side of the board, decide where you would like to hang items. They may be pictures, necklaces, cards etc. and mark. Hammer in a nail at each mark.

4. Attach the board to the wall. Attach your stationary clamp to pictures and hook on the nail. Hang any other trinkets on the spare nails.

5. Fill the gift bags with stationary, papers or any other items you wish. Not only does this look gorgeous on your wall but it also allows for wonderful memories and things you would like to do.

56. Storage Organizer Using Old Books

Materials

- Selection of old unused hardcover books
- Small box or wooden crate
- Hot glue gun
- Utility knife
- Scissors

Directions

1. Open the book and remove all pages leaving just the cover. Select which two books you want to place at either end. Cut out the spine of the books, ensuring that you leave a little space on one side to glue the next spine.

2. Glue each spine together with the next. Cut the one cover off the two books that you have left aside, leaving the other to frame your box on the side.

3. Glue the covers to your row of spines. Glue all the covers to your box. Fill your box with handy items such as pens, scissors and things you look for on a regular basis.

57. Revamp Filing Cabinet for Storage

Materials

- Old metal filing cabinet
- Sand paper
- Spray primer and paint
- Painter's masking tape
- Level (if making a decorative stripe)
- Casters (4 for a small and 6 for a large cabinet)
- Pencil
- Peg Board and peg board hanging kit
- Scrap wood
- Screws
- Power drill

Directions

1. Sand an old filing cabinet and wipe clean. Spray the cabinet with primer and allow primer to dry. Using a level mark where you want to put a decorative stripe and cover area with masking tape. Spray the rest of the cabinet and allow to completely dry.

2. Remove masking tape and cover the areas you have already painted with masking tape or newspaper. Spray your stripes; the paint must be dry before removing the tape. Measure the base of your cabinet and cut wood slightly smaller than the size of the base.

3. Place casters at equal intervals and mark the holes with a pencil (should be 2 inches from the edge of the board). Mark holes and screw casters to the board. Attach board to cabinet. Drill two holes through the board and base of cabinet and screw securely. Store your items from your garage like tools, drill kits, saws etc. in your new storage cabinet.

58. Soda Bottles Jewelry Stand

Materials

- 2 x 2 Liter Mountain Dew bottles
- 1 x 1 Liter Mountain Dew bottle
- 1 x 20 oz. Mountain Dew bottle
- Utility knife
- Scissors
- Threaded rod (12 inch)
- Drill
- Dermal tool
- Metal file

- Washers and nuts
- Glass bead
- Metal bead post
- Glue

Directions

1. Using the utility knife, cut the bottoms off the soda bottles and trim with scissors. Drill holes in the center of the bottle with a bit that is the same size as the threaded rod. If you want to hang bracelets on the bottom level, cut as far as you can between the 'petals' and smooth with the dermal tool. Smooth ragged edges with a file.

2. Turn one 2-liter bottom upside down and insert your rod, securing on both side with a washer and nut. Continue to thread the bases at intervals of your choice, each time securing with a washer and nut. At the top of the holder, glue a pretty bead. All that's left is to fill your new jewelry holder with all your necklaces, earrings and baubles.

59. PVC Beauty Tool Holder

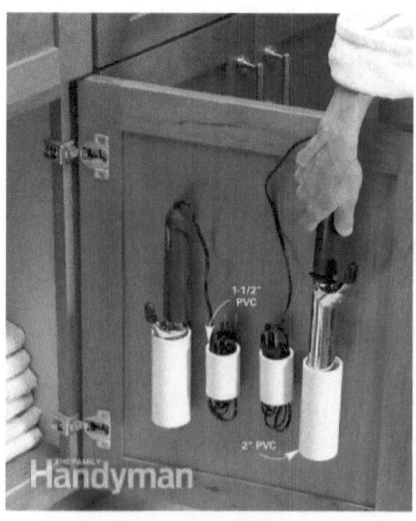

Materials

- PVC pipe (must have a vent and waste)
- Double sided tape

Directions

1. Find a suitable place next to your vanity. Secure the pipe to your wall. Place your hair dryer and curling tongs in each opening, leaving your dresser neat and tidy.

60. Handy Ribbon Dispenser

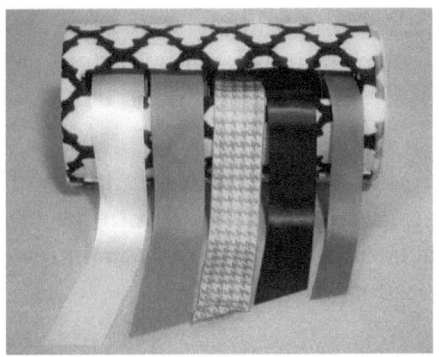

Materials

- Container (oatmeal Box)
- Fabric
- Scissors
- Ruler
- Tape measure
- Utility knife
- Spray adhesive
- Fabric glue
- Trim
- Dowel rod (length of container)

Directions

1. On your box draw a rectangle that is one-inch wide and cut out. Measure the height and circumference of the container. Mark size on the fabric, adding one inch all round and cut. Spray adhesive on to the box and gently wrap the fabric around the box, stopping just before the end. Fold the edge inwards and glue with fabric glue. Continue wrapping the fabric around the box and join with fabric glue.

2. Squeeze a line of glue inside the opening of the container and fold fabric over until secure. Draw a line along the center of the fabric that is covering the rectangle. Stop an inch short on either end and make a V. Cut the fabric along the line, apply glue to the edges and fold inside the box. Hold until the fabric is secure. Trace the lid of container onto fabric. Cut out and glue to the lid. Finish off the rough edges with trim.

3. Cut dowel rod to the size of the container. Thread your ribbon spools along the rod and insert into the container. Pull out a piece of each ribbon and now you know exactly what you when you need it.

61. Handy Trash Bag Roller

Materials

- 2 ¾ Inch curtain rod holders (can be bought in pairs)
- Wooden dowel (cut to size required)
- Spray paint (optional)
- Measuring tape
- Screwdriver
- Level
- Pencil
- Paper

Directions

1. Spray paint the dowels in a color of choice. Measure the size of dowel and mark on the wall. Drill two holes and insert wall plugs.

2. Insert dowel through the trash bag roll and hang between brackets. This is a great idea to hang under the sink or inside a closet door, making your bags handy and out of sight.

62. Nifty Fabric Organizer

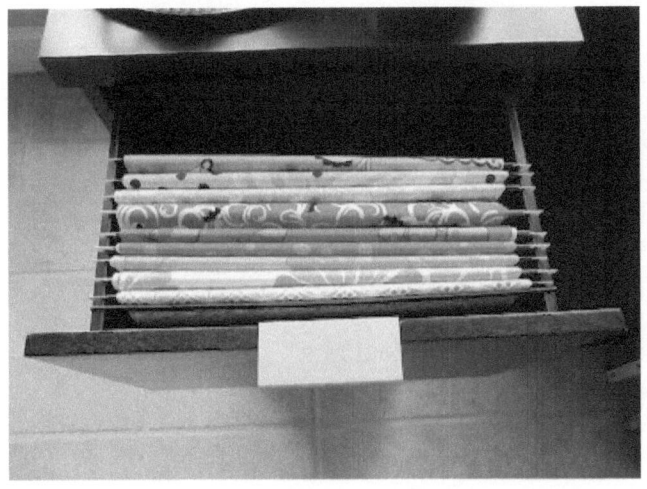

Materials

- Hanging files (size to fit filing cabinet or drawer)

Directions

1. Clear out a drawer. Hang your files in the drawer. Fold your fabrics into a rectangular shape. Put half the fabric in the file and loop the other half over the file. Now all your fabrics are stored in one place rather than having them cluttering up your closets.

63. Thread Rack Holder

Materials

- Balloon sticks
- Foam core
- Wrapping paper or fabric
- Grid paper (each block should be size of thread reel)
- Picture frame
- Hot glue gun
- Craft knife
- Craft spear (piercing tool)
- Mechanical pencil
- Double sided tape

Directions

1. Cut the foam core to match the size of the frame. Cover the foam with paper or fabric. Cut balloon sticks in 3-inch intervals. Place the grid paper over the fabric. Use the craft spear to punch a hole and widen slightly with the mechanical pencil so as to fit the balloon stick.

2. Squirt a dot of hot glue into hole; place stick inside and hold in place until the glue is set. Continue these steps until you have inserted all the balloon sticks. Place the rack into the frame and attach to the wall. Color co-ordinate all your threads along the sticks. No more tangled threads, saving you time and space.

64. Canned Food Organizer for Small Places

Materials

- 9 - 1 x 4" boards (cut to 29" pieces – top, bottom and shelves)
- 2 – 1 x 4" boards (cut to 64" pieces – side boards)
- 1 Thin board (cut to 31 ½ x 64" pieces – back board)
- 4 Metal casters – 2" to hold 50lbs+
- 7 x 7/16" Dowel rods (cut to 30" long)
- Handle
- Paint and roller or spray paint
- Wood filler

- Drill
- 7/16" Drill bit
- Wood screws
- 2" Nails
- Finishing nails
- Hammer

Directions

1. Place all the boards in the shape of a tall bookcase (top, bottom and sides). Use screws to build the outside shell walls, and nails on either side to attach the shelves. Measure 1 ½" from the bottom of each shelf and drill a hole through the outer boards. Insert dowels into holes. Paint your backboard (optional).

2. Attach the backboard using finishing nails. Fill holes and cracks with wood filler. Spray or paint the rest of the organizer. Attach casters as per the package directions. Attach handle. Fill the shelves with canned foods, spices, boxes of juice etc. Slide into place – you will be amazed at how much space you will save in your kitchen closets.

65. Craft Table with Storage Shelves

Materials

- 6 Pieces wood for shelves (1" by 12" by 32")
- 6 Pieces wood for top and bottom (1" x 12" x 49 1/8")
- 12 Pieces wood for sides (1" x 12" x 34 ¼")
- Laminated counter top as per your requirements
- Pieces of plywood to match the size of counter top.
- Kreg Jig
- Pocket screws
- Sand paper
- Primer
- Paint
- Nails
- Hammer

Directions

1. The material above will allow you to make three cubbies to support your table. Making pocket holes, attach two shelves to the sideboards. Attach the top board.

2. Attach two sideboards to the end of each shelf (on either side). Attach the bottom board. Sand the cubbies, paint with primer and allow to dry. Paint the cubbies in a color of choice. Depending of the size you want your table to be, order ready cut laminated counter top.

3. Cut strips of plywood to form the base of your laminated counter. This must match the layout of your cubbies and nail together.

4. Attach the counter to the plywood base. Baskets, bottles and tins can be used to store all your craft and art items on the shelves. If you have spare stools, slot underneath your table and the whole family can have fun around the table.

66. Quick and Easy Laundry Basket Closet

Materials

- Unused dresser
- Birch plywood
- Bead board
- Hinges
- Drill and bit
- Screws
- Door handles or knobs
- Laundry basket to fit
- Nails
- Hammer
- Sand paper
- Primer
- Semi-gloss paint

Directions

1. Measure the dimensions of the dresser. Cut plywood to make two doors as per requirements. Nail in bead wood to cover. Drill a hole in either door to attach handles or knobs.

2. Attach doors to frame. Measure the inside length of the dresser. Cut 2" plywood strips as per the length of dresser. On either side of the dresser, attach the plywood strip.

3. Sand the dresser and apply primer. Paint in color of choice. The top of the dresser can be painted in a different color to match bathroom counter tops. Slide the laundry baskets along the plywood support strips. Remind your family to put their dirty laundry into the baskets, leaving the bathroom floor neat and tidy.

67. Restored Drawer Storage Under Beds

Materials

- Unused dresser (if you don't have one at home, buy a cheap second hand one)
- Murphy's oil soap or suitable cleaner
- Primer
- Paint brush
- Sand paper
- Spray paint

- Scrapbook paper
- Mod podge
- Casters
- Drill
- Metal label holders
- Nails

Directions

1. Remove drawers from dresser and wash down. Sand the drawers, and paint with primer. Spray drawers with a color to match the room décor (sand in between layers). Spray 2 or 3 coats. Cut scrapbook paper according to the drawer measurements and cut. Brush the frame with mod podge and adhere paper. Paint two coats of mod podge over the paper.

2. Cover the drawer handles with scrapbook paper, using the same process above. Drill holes at the bottom of the drawer and attach the casters. Measure the length of the drawer and mark position of the metal label. Attach with small nails. Place a label into the metal holder with what is to go into each drawer. Pack the drawers with toys, shoes, magazines, books or any items that you are looking to store. Slide under the bed or a table, leaving you more space in your room or closets.

68. Covered Clothing Hangers

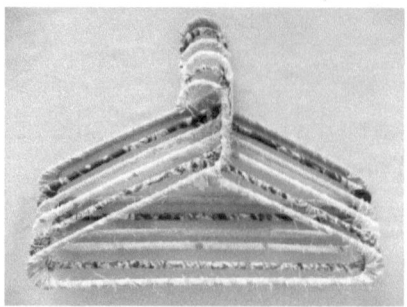

Materials

- Plastic hangers
- Jelly roll strips (various patterns)
- Scissors
- Score tape
- Nipper

Directions

1. Purchase plastic hangers (available in packs of 6). Cut off the small hooks inside the hanger. Cut the jellyroll in half (lengthwise).

2. Secure the fabric to the hanger with score tape, and tightly wrap the fabric around the hanger. As you wrap, secure the fabric with score tape at different intervals as well as at the end. The fabric-covered hangers will protect your clothing from hooking, as well as keep the shape of silk and fine materials.

69. Sewing Gadgets Organizer

Materials

- Scrap pieces of fabric
- Scrap pieces of complimentary fabric

- Embroidery hoop
- Fusible interfacing
- Needle and thread
- Metal rod per as per size requirements
- S shaped hooks
- Rod holders
- Screws and wall plugs
- Drill
- Iron

Directions

1. Cut outer fabric (14" height x 22" width). Add a layer of fusible interfacing. Fold fabric in half and sew a ½"seam along the side. Press seam open and sew another ½" seam at the bottom. Trim corners of bottom seam – V shape. Open the bag and pinch together the bottom corners. Sew a 4" seam across the corner to make a boxed bottom. Cut the corners off below the seam.

2. Turn the bag right side out. With the complimentary fabric, follow the above steps to make a lining for the bag. Insert the lining into the outer bag. Turn and sew a ½" seam towards the outside of the bag. One can use a fancy stitch to make it look attractive. Fold the top down towards the outside by 2". Insert the inner ring of the embroidery hoop under the folded edge.

3. Place the outer ring of the embroidery hoop over the fabric and join together with the inner hoop and tighten. Measure and mark the position of the metal rod. Attach the rod to the wall. Attach the bag to the S shaped hooks and hang on the metal rod. You can make more than one bag to hang on the rod and they become the perfect storage organizers for your wool, sewing utilities as well as odds and ends.

70. Fabric Covered Storage Boxes

Materials

- Wood to make shelves
- Brackets
- Screws and wall plugs
- Drill
- Old cardboard boxes
- Glue gun
- Spray paint
- Utility knife
- Mod podge
- Brush
- Fabric – to cover front of box
- Scissors

Directions

1. Decide how many boxes you want and cut the boxes according to the following sizes – bottom 10 x 9", 2 side pieces 11 x 10", front and back pieces 10 x 9". To assemble, glue the bottom piece to the inside bottoms of the front and back piece. Glue this section to the inside of the sidepieces.

2. Spray paint the sides and upper edges of the box in a color of your choice. Measure and mark a rectangle on the front of the

box. This will serve as a handle. Cut out the opening. Cut a piece of fabric slightly larger than the size of the front on the box. Apply mod podge to the box and lay the fabric onto the box, smoothing out all the lines and crinkles. Cut a slit in the opening for your handle, ending either side with a V. Fold over the pieces to the inside of the box and adhere with mod podge.

3. Wait for the mod podge to dry and trim off the fabric edges around the front of the box. Apply a second layer of mod podge on the fabric, making sure all the rough edges are secured. Allow to dry. Choose a suitable location and install your shelves, making sure that the brackets will fit in between boxes. Fill the boxes with supplies, spools of ribbons, wool and other accessories leaving you much needed space on your work counter.

71. Coat Rack Using a Chair Back

Materials

- Antique styled chair

- Saw
- Filigree hooks with attachments
- Saw
- Wood screws
- Screws and wall plugs
- Paint
- Brush
- Drill

Directions

1. Separate the back of the chair by cutting off the back legs.

2. Cut off the front legs of the chair but keep the base connecting the 2 legs. Mark the points where one will attach the legs to the back.

3. Drill holes and attach the legs to the chair back. Ensure that the screws are tightly fastened.

4. Paint the chair and legs. Along the strip between the legs attach the hooks.

5. Drill 2 holes on either side of the chair back. Find an appropriate spot in the hallway and mark where you intend to hang the coat rack.

6. Drill holes into the wall and insert the wall plugs.

7. Attach the coat rack to the wall, making sure that it is secure. Now your family can hang up their coats as they walk indoors instead of leaving them around your home causing more clutter.

72. Ladder Blanket Holder

Materials

- 2 x 6 Foot pieces of wood (1 x 4")
- ¾" Dowel rod (6 feet in length)
- Sand paper
- ¾" Paddle bit
- Screws
- Drill
- Wood stain (color of choice)
- Paint brush
- Paste finishing wax

Directions

1. Sand down the boards to give an old and rustic feel. Cut the dowel rods into 4 x 18" pieces. Lay the dowel pieces on the floor to work out where you would like the ladder rungs to be and mark on your wood.

2. Using the paddle bit drill a shallow round so that the dowel can slot in. Drill long screws into the board securing the dowel rods in place. Line up the second board and repeat the process above.

3. Wipe down the ladder and stain with a wood stain of your choosing. Once the ladder is dry, apply a coat of paste finishing wax. Fold blankets and throws over the rungs of your ladder. Now your blankets have a home that is neat, accessible to your family and at the same time you have saved space in your closets.

73. Hanging Display Rack for Shoes

Materials

- Spring tension rods (comes with attachments)
- Masking tape
- Tape measure
- Spirit level
- Drill

Directions

1. Find a suitable area in your bedroom, preferably a space between two walls. Using your show size as a guide, mark the spaces at intervals on either side of the wall. Drill holes and attach the tension rods.

2. Using masking tape, paste a strip across where the heels of your shoes would meet the wall. This prevents scuffmarks on the wall. Now you can color code your shoes and hang on the

tension cords. Not only will you be amazed at how beautiful it is look at but now you will save space in your closet and find your shoes without any hassle.

74. Decorating an Ottoman for Storage Space

Materials

- Cheap foldable or used ottoman
- Fabric of choice
- Staple gun
- Nail gun or drill and screws
- Hot glue gun
- Fabric covered button making kit
- Large needle and thread
- Pins
- Tassel
- Sewing machine

Directions

1. Remove the back part from the top of the ottoman. Flatten or remove the protruding nails. Measure the size of the top and cut your fabric accordingly. Cut the fabric 1" wider than required. Cover the top by stapling the fabric on making sure to fold the corners tightly and securely.

2. Cover a button with the fabric. With your needle, attach the button pulling the thread through the hole in the middle of the lid. Secure the thread. Attach your upholstered top to the backing board with screws or a nail gun. Open up the edge of the lining of the ottoman just enough to expose the staples.

3. Measure how much fabric you will require to cover the ottoman - width of ottoman + depth + 2-3" excess X height of ottoman + 4" excess. Cut material and hem the bottom part of the fabric. Wrap the fabric around the ottoman and pin. Make sure that the fabric fits snugly on the ottoman. Tip: fold the ottoman each time you want to remove the sleeve. Marking a guideline, sew the two sides together. Cut off excess fabric and iron the seam open.

4. Slip the fabric sleeve onto the ottoman making sure the hem line remains in line with the bottom of the ottoman. Fold over the fabric at the top and fold over again. Fold the fabric over the lip of the ottoman towards the inside and attach with staples to the edge at regular intervals.

5. Glue the lining back covering the staples. Hang a tassel or pretty necklace from the button making your ottoman giving it a sophisticated and glamorous look. Fill your ottoman with magazines or any other item you wish to store and place your bedroom or sitting room.

75. Simple Holder to Store Pot Lids

Materials

- Plastic adhesive hooks
- Tape measure
- Marker

Directions

1. Space out your pot lids in the inside of a cabinet door. Measure and mark the widest space between the lid and where it would rest on the hook. Stick an adhesive hook at each marking. Securely place pot lids between the hooks leaving you more cabinet space to store your pots and other items.

76. Handy PVC Shoe Rack

Materials

- PVC piping (150mm in diameter)

- Pipe glue or cement
- Brush
- Hacksaw
- Clothes pegs
- Sand paper

Directions

1. Cut PVC piping into pieces that would accommodate the biggest shoe size in your family. Sometimes the hardware store will cut for you otherwise you will have to use a hacksaw. Sand any rough edges and wash the pipes.

2. Align next to a wall and work out your stacking pattern. Brush glue along the pipe and attach one pipe to the next. Hold the two pipes together with a clothes peg until the glue is dry. Continue with this process until you have made sufficient shoe holders to accommodate the shoes in your closet. Place shoes in each holder and your children should have no excuse as to where to find their shoes.

77. Bathroom Jar Holders

Materials

- Pickle jars or other glass jars with lids in different sizes

- Grey primer
- Multi surface paint (assortment of colors)
- Paint brushes
- Pretty door knobs
- Glue

Directions

1. Wash the pickle jars a number of times to make sure they are clean and have left no trace of the pickling smell. Paint each lid with primer. Paint each lid 3 – 4 times as often it is difficult to cover the brand name of each lid. Allow the lids to dry for about 7 days.

2. Remove the bottom screw from the knobs and glue the knob to the middle of the lid. Leave to dry for another 24 hours. Fill the bottles with earbuds, cotton balls and cotton rounds. Not only do these bottles become a pretty bathroom accessory but makes it easier to have your everyday bathroom items close at hand instead of scratching through drawers.

78. Framed Table Organizer

Materials

- Picture frame
- Fabric

- Paper
- Glue
- Tape measure
- Pins
- Scissors
- Sewing machine or needle and thread

Directions

1. Purchase a picture frame with an ornate edge or if you have a spare one at home that can also be used. Open the frame and trace the shape of the backboard. Pin onto your fabric and cut. Measure the length of the backboard and divide into three sections. You are going to be making three pockets. Mark the measurements of each section on the paper as though you were making a pattern. Pin each section on the fabric and cut.

2. At the top of each pocket fold the edge of the material over and sew across. Taking the largest pocket, glue along the side and bottom edges. Attach to the backboard of frame. Do the same method for the other two pockets. Insert the board into the frame. Each pocket can now be filled with pens, paper and any other handy items that you would need at quick notice.

79. Easy Container to Store Hair Accessories

Materials

- Old oatmeal container
- Wrapping or craft paper
- Scissors
- Tape measure
- Scrapbook adhesive squares
- Candle stick holder (clear glass looks great)
- Hot glue gun
- Drawer knob

Directions

1. Remove the lid and take the measurements of the oatmeal container – height x circumference. Transfer these measurements to your wrapping paper and cut the shape of the container. Place the scrapbook adhesive to the back of the paper and then wrap the paper around the container.

2. Place scrapbook adhesives to the back of the paper and attach to the container. Place hot glue on the top part of your

candlestick holder and attach to the bottom of the container. Allow to dry.

3. Glue the drawer knob to the lid of the container. Fill your chic hair accessory container with bobby pins, clips, ribbons and other hair items. Now you really don't have to worry about losing your hair stuff anymore.

80. Storage Bin Using Recycled Tires

Materials

- Used tires (number depending on high you want the bin)
- 2 Pieces plywood
- Nuts and bolts
- Spray paint or paint
- Paint brush
- Casters and attachment kit
- Drawer handle
- Saw
- Tape measure
- Screws
- Drill
- Glue

Directions

1. Drill holes in the tires and attach together with the nuts and bolts. Paint the tires. Measure the width of the tires and cut two pieces of plywood as per the dimensions.

2. Glue the one piece of plywood to the base of the tires. Attach the casters to the base. Spray paint or paint the other piece of plywood, which will become the lid.

3. Glue the door handle to the middle of the top board. Find a location in your garden where your children love to play, and fill your new storage bin with toys. Alternatively, garden tools can be placed inside for easy use.

81. Turn A Diaper Box into A Closet Organizer

Materials

- Old diaper box
- Ribbons
- Sheets of pretty paper
- Ruler
- Tape measure

- Scissors
- Hot glue gun
- Metal label holder
- Paper
- Marker

Directions

1. Measure all the sides of the diaper box including the interior walls and the bottom. Lay out the paper and mark the measurements on the paper. If the sheet is big enough you can cut the paper in the shape of the box. Cut to size.

2. With the hot glue gun, carefully glue the edges of the paper to the sides of the box. Smooth out the paper s you go along and if the paper is patterned, try to keep the pattern in line and straight. Add the ribbon details to the box.

3. Centre the metal label holder and glue onto the box. Once you have decided what you are going to store, write the name of a piece of paper and insert into the holder. This can become a beautiful storage solution for linen and seasonal changes of clothes.

82. Space Saving Toilet Paper Holder

Materials

- Flower pot or planter
- Floral foam
- Dowel rod
- Cabinet knob
- Utility knife
- Glue

Directions

1. Use a spare flowerpot or planter or buy a cheap pot from the superstore. Cut the floral foam to fit into the pot. Insert the dowel rod into the floral foam.

2. Remove the screw from the knob and glue onto the end of the dowel rod. Simply stack extra toilet paper onto your new toilet holder and tuck into the corner. Now you will have extra space in your vanity for other things.

83. Create A Magazine Rack Using a Baby Crib

Materials

- Unused baby crib
- Old doors or plywood to measure
- 2 L-brackets and 2 flat braces (can recycle from the crib)
- Sand paper
- Hacksaw
- Screws
- Drill
- Tape Measure
- Marker
- Paint
- Paint brush

Directions

1. Either use your old baby crib or purchase one from a second-hand shop. Saw off the legs of the crib and sand smoothly. Measure the height and inside width of the crib. Cut a piece of plywood or doors according to the measurements. Place doors or board in the center of the crib and drill holes on all 4 sides of the crib, making sure that the screws are securely tightened.

2. Measure the height and width of the bottom of the crib and cut a piece of plywood or doors to these measurements (bottom shelf). Drill holes as above and attach to the crib securely. Using the legs that were cut off the crib; cut 4 smaller legs and attach to the bottom shelf. Use the L-brackets and braces to reinforce the legs.

3. Paint the magazine rack in a color of your choice. Place in a handy location and slip magazines over the top spindles and use the shelves to place books, plants or any other ornaments. Practical, functional and absolutely unique!

84. Gift Wrap Kitchen Stool Caddy

Materials

- Kitchen stool
- Sand paper
- Paint – color of your choice
- Brush
- 4 Casters and attachments
- Drill
- Scissors
- Old pillow cases
- Double sided Velcro
- Needle and thread

Directions

1. Purchase a second-hand kitchen stool or one of your own. Lightly sand the stool and paint. Attach the 4 casters to the top of the seat and flip over. Using your pillow cases make different sized storage bags.

2. Sew on a piece of double sided Velcro on either side on the bags. Cut a few extra pieces of Velcro to attach scissors, scotch tape etc.

3. Place your rolls of wrapping paper in the center of the stool and attach the storage bags to the center rungs of the stool – the longer bags and the top and the smaller bags below. Fill these bags with ribbons, tissue paper, gift tags, pens etc. Every time you need to wrap presents, wheel your gift-wrap caddy to the table and start wrapping. No longer will you have to search through drawers to find what you need.

85. Storage Boxes Made from Old Boxes and Sweaters

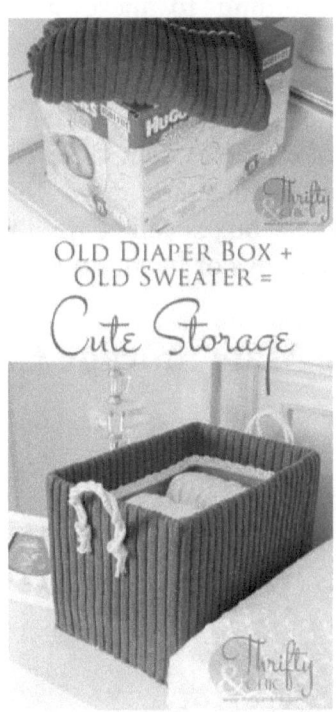

Materials

- Old boxes such as diaper boxes
- Sweater
- Utility knife
- Hot gun glue
- Ribbon
- Scissors
- Rope
- Measuring tape

Directions

1. Cut the flaps off the box. Measure the sides of the box and cut the sweater according to these measurements. Glue the sweater pieces to the side of the box, folding over a piece to the inside of the box. Finish off the raw edges with some ribbon. Cut 2 pieces of rope to make a handle. Twist the rope and make a knot on either end. Glue the rope handle onto the sweater. These handles are more for decoration than for practical use. These boxes can be used for a variety of storage ideas like diapers, toys or hand towels.

86. Coffee Mate Storage Containers

Materials

- Empty coffee mate containers
- Scissors
- Adhesive labels
- Marker

Directions

1. Collect your empty coffee creamer containers. Cut and peel off the label. Wash and thoroughly dry the container. On the labels write what you are going to store in each container and stick onto the container.

2. Fill each container with different food items such as nuts, popcorn kernels, chocolate chips, sprinkles, flour, sugar etc. The storage containers are a perfect size to fit in your pantry and if you really feel like having fun, decorate the outside of the container and use them at desert tables or ice cream sundae stations.

87. Recycle Pill Bottles to Handy Purse Storage Bottles

Materials

- Empty pill bottles
- Pretty paper

- Mod podge
- Glue
- Brush
- Scissors

Directions

1. Collect empty pill bottles. Wash the bottles and allow to dry well. Measure the dimensions of the bottle and cut your paper to the required size. Mixing mod podge and glue together, brush the mixture onto the back of the paper.

2. Gently wrap around the bottle, smoothing out as you go along. Paint the mod podge over the front of the paper and allowing it to dry. Take the lid of the bottle and trace onto a piece of paper.

3. Brush the mod podge and glue; brush onto the paper and paste onto the lid smoothing as you go. Apply another layer of mod podge. Fill your containers with earbuds, tweezers, toothpicks, band aids etc. and pop in your purse – what a handy travel item.

88. Practical Mason Jar Toothbrush Holder

Materials

- Mason Jar (wide mouth)
- Chicken wire
- Wire cutters

Directions

1. Remove the lid of the mason jar. Measure and cut the chicken wire to the same size as the round lid portion of the two-piece jar cap.

2. Add the chicken wire to the band of the lid and screw on the lid to your mason jar. Place the toothbrushes into the chicken wire and find an appropriate place on your bathroom dresser. Beautiful, smart and practical.

89. Hanging Enamel Mug Organizer

Materials

- 3 Large enamel mugs
- Piece of wood to fit
- Hand saw
- Wood varnish (optional)
- Brush
- Screws
- Glue
- Piece of chain
- Nail
- Hammer
- Drill
- Chalkboard stickers (optional)

Directions

1. Place your mugs on the wood to measure the correct size of the wood. The top mug will face upwards, and the bottom two will face outwards. Cut the wood to accommodate the mugs. The wood can be left as is or varnished or painted to match your color scheme.

2. Glue the top mug to the board. Drill a small hole in the middle of the other two mugs and attach to the wood. The middle mug's handle will face outwards and the bottom mug's handle will face downwards.

3. On either top corner of the wood, attach a piece of chain to hang the organizer. Your enamel mug organizer can be used in the kitchen to hold table linens; in the bathroom hand towels through the handles and other toiletry items. It is also great to use for holding craft supplies, stick on a chalkboard label and mark accordingly.

90. Creating Extra Space on Your Garage Ceiling

Materials

- 2 – 4 x 8" Wood
- 2 – 4 x 8" sheet of ¾" Plywood
- 1 – 2 x 8" Pine stop strip
- Carpenters glue
- ¼" x 3 ½" Lag screws and washers
- 2" Wood screws
- 3" Wood screws
- 6 – 23 ½" x 19 ½" x 13" Plastic totes or size of choice
- Tape measure
- Drill
- Wood bit
- Stud finder
- Snap chalk

Directions

1. If not using the tote bags suggested in the materials, measure the width of the tote rims and the bottom size of the flanges of

the carriages. Cut 3" wide strips of ¾" plywood for the bottom flange. Centre them on the 4-foot-long 2x4", glue and screw together. Use the 2" screws every 10".

2. Flip the carriage assemblies over. Centre the 5" wide plywood top flanges and glue and screw them together. This would complete the carriage assemblies. Locate the ceiling joists with a stud finder and mark lines with snap chalk. Probe with a finish nail to ensure the lines fall on joist centers.

3. Mark each carriage 12" from the end and align the mark with the joist location. Screw the carriage temporarily to each joist on one side of the flange with 3" screws.

4. Cut a 2x4" template from your tote dimensions and mark the location of the top edge of the next carriage.

5. Mark the rear side as well; then screw it and the other carriages in place on one side only. Check the fit of the totes and make sure the rims have maximum bearing on the lower flanges. Make any necessary adjustments.

6. Drill 3 16" pilot holes in the top flanges. Then drive pairs of 3 ½" lag screws into each joist, removing the temporary screws as you go. Use a minimum of 4 lag screws per carriage.

7. Mark the centers of the carriages and screw a 2" pine stop strip along the marks. The stop will prevent the totes from falling to far into the carriages.

8. These tote bags are perfect for lightweight storage or bulky items that would usually take up a lot of space in your garage area. The rims of these containers will support a weight of 35 lbs. or more but the total weight of all the totes should not exceed 210 lbs.

91. Magnetic Makeup Board Holder

Materials

- Picture frame
- Spray paint
- Glaze
- Brush
- Piece of metal to fit inside frame
- Spray adhesive
- Fabric
- Small magnets
- Hot glue gun

Directions

1. Purchase a picture frame or buy one from a second-hand store. Remove the picture, and spray paint the frame. Paint the frame with glaze. Ask the hardware store to cut a piece of metal the size of the backing board of the frame.

2. Cut the fabric to the size of the metal board. Spray adhesive to the metal and stick on the fabric, gently smoothing to eliminate bubbles and lines.

3. Place the board into your frame. Hot glue the magnets to the back of eye shadow containers. Arrange your eye shadows on your frame and either keep on your vanity or hang on the wall in an accessible spot.

92. Washi Tape Organizer

Materials

- Clear drawer organizer
- 2 x Tension rods
- Serrated edges from two plastic wrap boxes
- Double sided tape
- Metal label holder
- Paper
- Marker

Directions

1. Remove the serrated edges from the plastic wrap boxes. Run hot water over the edges to remove any glue and cardboard. Cut the double-sided tape into thin strips and attach the serrated edges to the top lip of the drawer.

2. Fit the tension rods into the drawer. Slide the rolls of washi tape on the rods, making sure that the tape unfolds towards the edge of the organizer. Place the end of the washi tape on the serrated edge.

3. Attach a metal label holder on the front of the box and label. This nifty organizer will make your crafting area neater plus you will know exactly what washi tape you have available to craft with.

93. Pencil and Pen Holders

Materials

- Glass jars with lids
- Paint
- Old newspapers

Directions

1. Collect your empty jelly or jalapeno jars. Clean and wash the jars thoroughly. Make sure that you buy paint that is able to stick to glass, if water based you can dilute if too thick.

2. Pour some paint into the jar, close and swirl the paint around the sides of the jar. Pour the excess paint back into the paint tin. Leaving the jar on, tip the bottle upside down and allow the excess paint to drip into the lid (overnight).

3. Wipe the excess paint from the lid of the jar and leave to dry. This can take a few days. Fill your new holders with pens, pencil and paint brushes. They are also very handing to store makeup brushes.

Conclusion

Making your home clutter free can be a tough and time taking task. You can easily reduce your burden by simply using the crafts discussed in this book to make your home more organized and manageable.

Although some of the crafts discussed in this book are time taking and you might find them a little difficult, but trust me, each of these crafts will be worth your effort and time. By using these simple techniques your messy and unorganized house can be converted into a clean, neat and an organized home.

These simple crafts will help you save time and energy because it will be much easier to organize your things. These crafts are so designed that you don't have to take extra time out from your daily routine in order to be organized and systematic.

Once you get used to these wonderful pieces of magic, your life would seem a turmoil to you without them. So, get your hands dirty and start making these handy little things, which will make your life easy and comfortable.

Last Chance to Get YOUR Bonus!

FOR A LIMITED TIME ONLY – Get my best-selling book "DIY Crafts: The 100 Most Popular Crafts & Projects That Make Your Life Easier" absolutely FREE!

Readers who have downloaded the bonus book as well have seen the greatest changes in their crafting abilities and have expanded their repertoire of crafts – so it is *highly recommended* to get this bonus book today!

Get your free copy at:

ArtsCraftsAndMore.com/Bonus

Final Words

Thank you for downloading this book!

I really hope that you have been inspired to create your own projects and that you will have a lot of fun crafting.

I do hope that you and your family have found lots of ways to fill lazy afternoons or rainy days in a more fun way.

If you have enjoyed this book and would like to share your positive thoughts, could you please take 30 seconds of your time to go back and give me a review on my Amazon book page!

I really appreciate these reviews because I like to know what people have thought about the book.

Again, thank you and have fun crafting!

Disclaimer

No Warranties: The authors and publishers don't guarantee or warrant the quality, accuracy, completeness, timeliness, appropriateness or suitability of the information in this book, or of any product or services referenced by this site.

The information in this site is provided on an "as is" basis and the authors and publishers make no representations or warranties of any kind with respect to this information. This site may contain inaccuracies, typographical errors, or other errors.

Liability Disclaimer: The publishers, authors, and other parties involved in the creation, production, provision of information, or delivery of this site specifically disclaim any responsibility, and shall not be held liable for any damages, claims, injuries, losses, liabilities, costs, or obligations including any direct, indirect, special, incidental, or consequences damages (collectively known as "Damages") whatsoever and howsoever caused, arising out of, or in connection with the use or misuse of the site and the information contained within it, whether such Damages arise in contract, tort, negligence, equity, statute law, or by way of other legal theory.

www.ingramcontent.com/pod-product-compliance
Lightning Source LLC
Chambersburg PA
CBHW031125080526
44587CB00011B/1109